Fully Persuaded

Nothing Can Separate Us From the Love of God!

Rudi Louw

Copyright © 2014 by Rudi Louw Publishing

All rights reserved solely by the author. No part of this book may be reproduced in any form *without the permission of the author.*

Most Scripture quotations are taken from the RSV®, *Revised Standard Version*, Copyright © 1983 by Thomas Nelson, Inc.

Some Scripture quotations were taken from the NKJV, *New King James Version*, Copyright © 1983 by Thomas Nelson, Inc.

And some Scripture quotations were taken from the Mirror Bible, Copyright © 2012 by Francois du Toit.

The Scripture quotations not taken from the RSV, NKJV and Mirror Bible are a *literal translation* of the Scriptures.

The Holy Scriptures are just that, HOLY.

Statements enclosed in brackets were inserted into Scripture quotations to add emphasis or to clarify the meaning of what is being said in those scriptures. The integrity of God's Word to man was not compromised in any way. Due care and diligence was cautiously exercised to keep the Word of Truth intact.

Table of Content

The Marvel of the Holy Bible 5

Acknowledgment 11

Foreword 13

Prayer 21

1. *God Knows Who We Are!* 27
2. *All Ministry Flows From the Love of God!* 39
3. *Life More Abundantly!* 45
4. *Treasure In the Face of Christ* 51
5. *Applying The Treasure!* 59
6. *Hinds' Feet on High Places* 67
7. *The Glorious Liberty of the Children of God* 71
8. *God Is For Us! Not Against Us!* 77
9. *Hold Fast The Confession Of Your Faith!* 89
10. *Give the Devil No Place!* 101
11. *The Immeasurable Love of Jesus!* 107
12. *Maintaining a True Heart* 111

13. *The Fellowship of the Saints* *119*
About the Author *133*

The Marvel of the Holy Bible

1. Uninterrupted Theme and Inspired Thought

It took *1,500 years* to compile the Holy Bible, involving *more than 40 different authors*. <u>Yet</u> the theme and inspired thought of Scripture, continues *uninterrupted* from author to author, from beginning till end.

2. Absence of Mythical Stories

Compare philosophies and theories about creation in the Middle East, Europe, Asia, Africa, and Latin America and you'll find mythical scenarios: gods feuding and cutting up other gods to form the heavens and the earth, etc.

In ancient Greek mythology, the Greeks see Atlas carrying the earth on his shoulders. In India, Hindus believe eight elephants carry the earth on their backs.

But in contrast, Job, the oldest book in the Holy Bible, declares that, *"God suspends the earth 'on nothing."(Job 26:7)*

This was said millennia before Isaac Newton discovered the invisible laws of gravity that delicately balance every planet and sun in its individual circuit.

Contrary to every other ancient attempt to give a creation account, *the Holy Bible pictures the creation of the earth in a very scientific manner.*

Example: In Genesis Chapter One, the continents are lifted from the seas then vegetation is formed and later animal life all reproducing *'according to its own kind',* **thus recognizing the fixed genetic laws.** In addition, we have the bringing forth of man and woman, *all done by God in a dignified and proper manner, without mythological adornments.*

The balance or remainder of the Holy Bible follow suite.

The narratives are **true historical documents**, *faithfully reflecting society and culture* **as history and archaeology would discover them thousands of years later. Not only is the Holy Bible historically accurate, it is also reliable when it deals with scientifically proven subjects.**

It was never intended to be a textbook on history, science, mathematics, or medicine. *However, when its writers touch on these subjects,* **they often state facts that scientific advancement would not reveal, or** *even consider, until thousands of years later.*

While many have doubted the accuracy of the Holy Bible, time and continued research have consistently demonstrated that the Word of God is better informed than its critics.

3. Intactness

Of all the ancient works of substantial size, *the Holy Bible survives intact, against all odds and expectations.*

Compared with other ancient writings, the Holy Bible has more manuscripts as evidence to support it than any ten pieces of classical literature combined!

The plays of William Shakespeare, for instance, were written about four hundred years ago, after the invention of the printing press. Many of his original writings and words have been lost in numerous sections, *yet the Holy Bible's uncanny preservation, has weathered thousands of years of wars, contradictions, persecutions, fires and invasions.*

Through the centuries Jewish scribes have preserved the Holy Bible's Old Covenant text, **such as no other manuscripts has ever been preserved. They kept tabs on every letter, syllable, word and paragraph.** They *continued from generation to generation to appoint and train special groups of men within their culture,* **whose sole duty it was to preserve and transmit these documents, <u>with perfect accuracy and fidelity</u>.**

Who ever bothered to count the letters, syllables, or words of Plato, Aristotle, or Seneca for that matter?

When it comes to the New Testament, the actual number of preserved manuscripts is so great that it becomes overwhelming. **There are more than 5,680 Greek manuscripts, more than 10,000 Latin Vulgate manuscripts and at least 9,300 other versions. Further still, there exists an additional 25,000 manuscript copies of portions of the New Testament.** No other document of antiquity even begins to approach such numbers.

The closest in comparison is Homer's <u>Iliad</u>, with only 643 manuscripts. The first complete work of Homer only dates back to the 13th century.

4. Unmatched Accuracy in Predictive Foretelling

The Holy Bible is unmatched in accuracy in predictive foretelling. No other ancient work succeeds in this, or even begins to attempt this.

Other books, such as the Koran, the Book of Mormon, and parts of the Veda claim divine inspiration; *but none of these books contain predictive foretelling.*

This one undeniable fact we know for certain: *While microscopic scrutiny would show up the imperfections, blemishes and defects of any work of man, it magnifies the beauties and perfection of God. Just as every flower displays in accurate detail the reflection and perfection of beauty, so does the Word of Truth when it is scrutinized.*

Historian Philip Schaff wrote:

"Without money and weapons, Jesus the Christ conquered more millions, than Alexander, Caesar, Mohammad, and Napoleon. Without science and learning, He (Jesus the Christ) shed more light on things human and divine than all philosophers and scholars combined. Without the eloquence of schools, He (Jesus the Christ) spoke such words of life as was never spoken before or since and produced effects which lie beyond the reach of orator or poet. Without writing a single line, He (Jesus the Christ) set more pens in motion and furnished themes for more sermons, orations, discussions, learned volumes, works of art, and songs of praise ***than the whole army of great men of ancient and modern times combined.****"* (*The Person of Christ*, p33. 1913)

Today, there are literally billions of Bibles in more than 2,000 languages.

Isn't it about time you find out what it really has to say?

Hey listen, the Holy Bible is all about Jesus, the Messiah, the Christ…

…and everything about Jesus Christ is really about YOU!!

Study Tips:

Read 2 Corinthians 5:14, 16, 18, 19, and 21.

In the light of these Scriptures, it should be obvious that, if you want to study the Holy Bible, *you should study it in the light of mankind's redemption!*

Feed daily on redemption realities found in the book of Acts, in Romans Chapters One through Eight, and in Ephesians, Colossians, and Galatians, also in 1 Peter Chapter One, 2 Peter Chapter One, James Chapter 1, as well as in 1 and 2 Corinthians.

Acknowledgment

I want to acknowledge and thank one of my mentors in the faith, Francois du Toit, for blessing and impacting me with revelation knowledge.

I borrowed the portion on *"The Marvel of the Holy Bible"* from his website, http://www.MirrorWord.net, as students so often feel they have a right to do with things that come from teachers they respect. Just as Galatians 6:6 says, *"Let him who is taught the Word **share in all good things** with him who teaches."*

To all our dear friends and family, and to Chase Aderhod who helped me with this project, but especially:

To my wife, Carmen

For all the love and support, and for being my partner in ministry, standing strong with me through thick and thin, even in the face of many trials and severe contradiction at times.

THANK YOU!

I love and appreciate you so very much!

Foreword

Thank you for taking the time to read this book.

Let me start off by saying that *I am totally addicted to my Daddy's love for me.*

I am in love with Jesus Christ, *and that is enough for me!*

The love of God is so much more than a doctrine, a philosophy, or a theory. It is so much more and goes so much deeper than knowledge: *it way surpasses knowledge.*

We are talking heart language here.

I write *to impact people's hearts,* to make them see the mysteries that have been hidden in Father God's heart concerning Christ Jesus, and really *concerning THEM.* I do this so as to arrest their conscience with it, *that I may introduce them to their original design and their true selves,* **presenting them to themselves perfect in Christ Jesus,** *and thereby setting them apart unto Him* **in love***,* as a chaste virgin.

We are involved with the biggest romance of the ages!

Therefore this book cannot be read as you would a novel: *casually.* It is not a cleverly devised little myth or fable. **It contains revelation and *truth* about some things you may or may not have considered before.**

It is the TRUTH of God, ultimate TRUTH, and therefore has direct bearing upon YOUR life. The Word and the Spirit are my witness *to the reality of these things!*

Be like the people of Berea whom the Apostle Paul ministered to in Acts 17:11. Open yourself up to study the revelation contained in this book, **to discover for yourself the reality of these things.**

Be forewarned, and do not become guilty of the sins of the Pharisees, **or you too will miss out on the depth of fulfillment God Himself, who is LOVE, wants to give <u>YOU</u>.**

Jesus said of the Pharisees and Sadducees that they strain out every little gnat BUT swallow whole camels. What He meant by that is that *some people seem to have it all together when it comes to doctrine and they love to argue.*

It makes them feel important but it is nothing other than EMPTY religious and intellectual pride.

They know the Scriptures in and out and YET they are still so IGNORANT about **REAL TRUTH that is only found in LOVE.** *They are still so ignorant and indifferent* **towards the things that REALLY MATTER.** They are always arguing over the use of *every little jot and tittle* and over the meaning and interpretation of *every word of Scripture.*

The exact thing they accuse everyone else of doing though, the precise thing they judge everyone else for, *they are actually doing themselves.* That is, **they often completely misinterpret and twist what is being said,** *making a big deal of insignificant things, while obscuring or weakening God's real truth: the truth of His LOVE.*

They are always majoring on minors **<u>because they do not understand the heart of God</u>***, and therefore they constantly miss the whole point of the message.*

Paul himself said it so beautifully,

"…the letter kills but **the Spirit BRINGS LIFE***…"*

"…<u>knowledge puffs up</u>, but **LOVE EDIFIES***…"*

I say again:

Allow yourself to get caught up in the revelation I am about to share.

Open yourself up to study the insight contained in this book, *not only with a desire to gain knowledge, but also with anticipation* **to hear from Father God yourself***,* **to encounter Him through His Word, and to embrace truth in** *order to know and believe the LOVE God has for <u>you.</u>*

*Get so caught up in it **that you too may receive from Him LOVE'S impartation of LIFE.***

*If you take heed to these things and yield yourself fully to it, **it is custom designed and guaranteed to forever alter and enrich your life!***

"What shall we say
of all of these things
that come against us?

If God is for us,
who can be against us!"

"He who did not spare
His own life,
but gave himself up
for us all,
will He not also,
with Christ Jesus,
give us all things?"

"Who then
shall bring any charge
against God's elect?

It is God Himself
who justifies them!"

"Who is there to condemn?

Is it Christ Jesus
who died,
and furthermore
was raised from the dead
and is even now

at the right hand of God, our ever living intercessor?"

"What can separate me from the love of Christ?

Shall tribulation, or distress, or persecution, or famine, or nakedness,

or peril,
or sword?"

"NO!

In **all**
these things
we are
more than conquerors

through Him
who loves us!"

~ Romans 8:31-37

Prayer

Father, we thank you that we may know that every morning the steadfast love of the Lord is new and fresh.

Thank you for a fresh quickening of the spirit within us.

Thank you that our spirits are quickened within us by the indwelling of Your Spirit, Lord.

Thank you, Father, that we are no longer as a wilted plant, because You have moistened us through and through with Your love. Daddy God, You have drenched us and saturated us with the dew from heaven.

Thank you, Father, that You lift our spirits, that You encourage us afresh and anew today.

Thank you, Father, that You have called the *'Church',* the body of Christ, the community of believers, into fellowship with Yourself, so that out of that encounter and intimate fellowship with You we can encourage and strengthen each other so that together we may all remain strong in the Lord and in the power of His might, endued with power from on high, strengthened together in our inner-man, that Christ may continue to dwell and live large in our hearts and within our lives.

Thank you, Father, that we can indeed be a blessing to one another as we live in Your presence.

As we drink from Your love we begin to reflect into the atmosphere the reality of the conviction of our hearts: that Jesus Christ is alive and well, that He is indeed the resurrection and the life, that He has raised us from the dead, from a dull and dreary existence, to a life of vitality.

Thank you, Father, that we can be alive in the spirit today, that we can honor You, Father, that we can honor You, Jesus, that we can live a life of enthusiasm, a vibrant life; life more abundantly!

I thank you, Father, for the blessing that is reflected through our lives, and is emanating from us and having an impact in our surroundings.

Thank you that together with other believers we can draw from that strength that is ours in Christ Jesus.

And Father, we thank you that as we open the Scriptures together in this book, that the Holy Spirit opens our understanding to receive revelation upon revelation, so that our hearts will be set ablaze with Your love and Your purpose.

And, Father, I thank you that we are all being thrust forth in this day with a new zeal into our daily lives and into this world.

Father, as we go out into the world as ministers of Your gospel, we do not take the truth of the gospel lightly. Father, we never want to make light of Your gospel, ever, Father. What a tremendous gospel, what an enormously beautiful work of redemption You accomplished in Christ!

Father, and now we also want to covenant with You that we will not take these things lightly, we will not take Your commission lightly, we will not receive revelation knowledge into these things of the gospel, just for ourselves. But we will go forth and be the fountain that You have called us to be so that others can drink from us, Lord, and be saved, so that they would have their thirst quenched and be thirsty no more as we begin to communicate to them with clarity of what we have heard, of what we have seen, of what we have beheld, what we have touched and handled and made our own, of Your love and of Your sweetness, and of Your very presence.

Thank you, Father, that others will come into the same fellowship we enjoy with You, and into the same manifestation of Your glory.

Thank you, Father, that we will see other people's lives transformed. Alcoholics and drug addicts and other people that live their lives in misery and pain, as well as people whose marriages are falling apart and businesses are crumbling.

I thank you that we have been entrusted with the reality of Your life and Your very person, that we have a message of life and liberty and victory, oh God!

And I so thank you, Father, that we do not have to be professional people *before we can qualify to reach others,* God. I thank you that we don't need to be theologians and clergymen with degrees. *We just need to be a people who walk in the reality of Jesus.*

I thank you that the truth of the gospel is powerful on our lips, Father God. I thank you that Your Word is as powerful in our mouths and on our lips as it was on the lips of Jesus, as it was even in Your own mouth when You created out of nothing, when You said, *"Light be!"* and light was.

I thank you that You have placed that authority in our mouths, Father God. So that as we speak, Father, it might seem to ourselves and to others so insignificant compared to the excellence of human wisdom, but I thank you that You have chosen the foolishness of what we preach, of what we proclaim and share, to penetrate people's hearts with Your love and Your reality, and to demonstrate Your very power, oh God!

I thank you that the power of God is demonstrated this very day, even in this book and because of this book, as I share your Word, as I bring forth an utterance that is from

God, and as we fellowship together with Your Spirit in these truths.

And I thank you, Father, that as we move on from this time together in this book and go our different ways into the future, Your voice will be the thing that is extended to others through our lips and amplified in our lives, and your Word, Your gospel truth, continues to prosper in its purpose.

In the Mighty Name of Jesus!

Amen.

Chapter 1

God Knows Who We Are!

It is such a wonderful thing to get caught up in the Spirit of God *and lose track of time altogether…* ha… ha… ha…

I am so glad that eternity is not bound by time. *It is outside of time and space and it rules time and space, hallelujah!* I'm so thankful that we have become partakers of that eternal life, life in relational bliss with God, life in the spirit dimension, in the spirit realm, amen! And that intimacy with God, that realm, that life, is not bound by time, amen!

So go ahead, it's okay: Lose track of time and get caught up in the Spirit while meditating and pondering upon the things in this book… ha… ha… ha. .

I am so glad that time was invented to serve us, not the other way around. *We are not slaves to time, thank you Jesus!* I am so glad that we may all now, in the light of the gospel, *escape our time-bondage thinking.*

Before we begin with our study together in this book, I want you to just quickly make this confession out loud with me:

I have a real expectancy in my heart right now!

I am not sure where to start with this teaching because all the Scriptures are so interconnected. This whole Bible says the same thing, amen. And when one begins to grasp that common theme, it is difficult to start reading anywhere in Scripture without many scripture verses and passages bearing strong witness together with the Holy Spirit within you, all at the same time, amen.

I mean that, when we speak, we speak from the whole volume of the book, amen. And sometimes it is hard to know where to end, or how to stop, because it's a big book without any brakes… ha… ha… ha…

I really want to get to 2 Corinthians Chapter Four, but let's start by taking a look at 2 Corinthians 5:10 & 11 first,

"For we must all appear before (face) the judgment seat of Christ, so that each one may receive (evaluate) good or evil, according to what he has done in the body."

"Therefore knowing the fear of the Lord, we persuade Men; but what we are is known to God, and I hope it is also known to your conscience."

Some translations even go as far as to say,

"Knowing therefore the terror of the Lord, we persuade men..."

I really believe that that word **fear** was mistranslated in most Bibles when somewhere in the course of time someone mistakenly used the wrong Greek word in rewriting Paul's letters and therefore mistranslated this scripture *and messed up the interpretation of it for all the rest of us.* And later when it was translated into the English language from the Latin, instead of fixing the error, *the mistranslation was perpetuated* because of the heavy law and judgment mindsets of the original King James translators.

Even when the difference between the two Greek words in question was pointed out to them, the correct Greek word was thrown out in preference for the word *fear* which more closely corresponds to their interpretation of things and their view of God which was heavily influenced by the Greek philosopher Aristotle, and the image of Zeus found in Greek mythology.

It is imperative that we get a more accurate picture of what the Holy Spirit though Paul is really saying here in this scripture. I personally feel that the Mirror Bible brings that out the best *by using the more correct Greek word, the one Paul most likely originally used in this passage.*

The Mirror Bible puts it so beautifully,

"**5:10 For we have all been** 1 **thoroughly scrutinized in the** 2 **footsteps of Jesus** *(not as an example for us but of us)* **and are** 3 **taken care of and restored to the life of our design, regardless of what happened to us in our individual lives, whatever amazing or meaningless things that we encountered in the body.** *(The word* 1 ***phaneroo****, means to render apparent, to openly declare, to manifest. Paul uses the aorist passive infinitive tense **phanerothenai**, <u>not referring to a future event</u>.* **The aorist tense is like a snapshot taken of an event <u>that is already concluded</u>.** *The word,* ***bematos****, comes from* 2 ***bayma****, meaning footprint, also referring to a raised place mounted by steps, or a tribunal, the official seat of a judge. The word* 3 ***komitzo****, comes from **kolumbos**, meaning to tend, to take care of, to provide for, to carry off from harm. Paul's reference was not how much abuse and affliction he suffered, neither was it the many good times he remembered that defined him, he said: "I am what I am by the grace of God!"* **If we are still to be judged for good or bad deeds that we performed in the body, then the judgment that Jesus faced on humanity's behalf seems irrelevant.***)*

5:11 We persuade people in the 1 **radiance of the Lord! His visible glory is mirrored in us! Our lives are transparent before God; we anticipate that you will witness the same transparency in your own** 2 **conscience!**
(The word, 2 ***suneido****, translates as*

*conscience, in Latin it means to know together; and in the Greek, it translates as joint seeing; which is the opposite of **hades**, not to see. In 2 Corinthians 4:2 we read, "With the open statement of the truth we commend ourselves to everyone's conscience." The word **phobe**, speaks of dread, terror, and fear! I would prefer to use the word, 1 **phoibe**, which means radiant! Now that sounds more typical of the God of Creation who unveiled himself in Christ! Jesus is the express image of God, the radiance of His beauty! He has made the invisible God visible! He is the Father of lights with whom there is no shadow due to compromise; there is no dark side to God! To persuade people in fear is in total contrast to what Paul's ministry was all about! See in 2 Corinthians 5:14, the love of Christ persuades me that one has died for all; this can only mean that all, in fact, were equally included in his death!)"*

It is amazing how one small little word as **phoibe,** mistranslated into **phobe** can lead to such a mess in people's theology ha…ha…ha…

Even if we leave the word, **phobe** intact as it is in this text, Paul could be saying: *"Knowing therefore **this religious mentality people have; this wrong legalistic mentality of dread and terror and fear that keeps prevailing concerning God,** we **persuade** men **otherwise**; we **persuade** people **contrary to it!**"*

*"...**Because who we really are is known to God,** and so my hope is that it is also therefore known to your conscience."*

In other words, God knows us intimately, we are His children and He loves us! He always has and He always will. He proved that He would rather face judgment Himself, than to judge us. He proved that He would rather die and go to hell Himself in our place, than to live without us! He is that much in love with us!

I want to take one sentence there, in 2 Corinthians Chapter Five, Verse 11 in the Mirror Bible that stands out to me, and I want to use that as our theme in this book. In the RSV it is reduced to a short statement. Paul says there,

*"Therefore knowing the fear of the Lord, **we persuade men**. But what we are is known to God, and I hope it is also known to your conscience."*

The Mirror Bible adds so much depth to that statement,

5:11 We persuade people *in the radiance of the Lord!* His visible glory is mirrored in us! Our lives are transparent before God; we anticipate that you will witness the same transparency in your own conscience!

Paul says, ***"We persuade people in the radiance of the Lord!"***

And then he says, *"**His visible glory is mirrored in us!**"*

He goes on to say there in the RSV,

*"…**What we are is known to God,** and I hope it is also known to your conscience."*

Paul has a whole discourse with these folks who live in the city and region around Corinth. He is defending his ministry because people have started kicking and knocking his ministry down by speaking against him. He actually starts off in Chapter Two saying,

"Are we beginning to commend ourselves again?"

People sometimes judge a ministry in the natural and they try and criticize it and break it down and write it off, because the enemy is contradicting the ministry in their minds, and trying to use them to contradict the ministry in other people's minds as well, in order to cause that ministry to lose its integrity and impact upon Men's hearts and lives. There is nothing the enemy desires more than to contradict the integrity of the Word of God, *the integrity of the gospel* in people's hearts and minds. So his strategy is to throw all kinds of accusations and criticisms and ideas out there as an accusation and a contradiction against the integrity of someone's ministry of the gospel, especially someone like Paul.

So Paul, in defense of his ministry says here in 2 Corinthians 5:11,

*"We are not trying to commend ourselves. What we are is known to God, **but in our ministry, we persuade people…"***

So I want us to consider *that theme* in our study together of the Scriptures in this book, **because God wants to persuade people;** God wants to bring people to the place where the truth of the gospel so convicts them, so impacts and overwhelms them in their hearts *with a conviction and a persuasion of His love and reality,* that that truth, that revelation, will totally liberate them. God in His love wants His people to be a free people, **so we persuade people in the truth of the gospel,** because Jesus said in John 8:32,

*"You will know the truth (the truth of the gospel), and **the truth will set you free!***"

2 Corinthians 3:17 & 18 says,

*"**Now the Lord is the Spirit,** and where the Spirit of the Lord is, **there is freedom**."*

This scripture can also be read as saying,

*"Now the Lord is the Spirit, and **where the Spirit is Lord, there is freedom**."*

"And we all now, with unveiled faces, beholding the glory of the Lord, are being changed into His likeness, from one glory to

another. **This comes from the Lord who is the Spirit**."

I want you to notice that it says that,

*"…we all, **with unveiled face**…"*

Meaning, **we all who are living** *in the reality of Verse Seventeen,*

*"…**In the freedom of the Spirit**,"*

Where the Spirit has freedom to demonstrate the glory of Jesus,

*"…**we are being changed**,"* he says.

That means nothing less than **we are being persuaded.** You cannot be changed **until you are persuaded!** We are being persuaded **by the revelation of the integrity of God's love.** We are being persuaded **by that revelation, by the integrity of the revelation of God's glory.**

That means we suddenly realize that there is more value, more worth *in the revelation of the love of God, in the revelation of the glory of God, than in all my ambitions that I had in this world put together.* Suddenly, I begin to see my life; my life in this world and the lives of every individual in this world, *from another point of view.* And now I begin to agree with Paul that, ***whatever gain I had, I now count it as a loss, as refuse, in comparison with the excellence of the knowledge of Jesus.***

You see, nothing else will persuade people for the gospel of Jesus Christ and for the kingdom of God *but the revelation of God's love, God's glory!* It is not through clever arguments and clever theological debates and discussions. But what will persuade people is *the love of God.* **What will persuade people is the very reflection of the glory of Jesus *in our testimony.***

In 2 Corinthians 6:1 Paul writes,

"Working together with Him then, we entreat you not to receive the grace of God in vain."

He says,

*"I am writing to you Corinthians, **that you will not be otherwise persuaded."***

That means **persuaded by your criticisms and by other people's opinions about the integrity of our ministry to you, *about the truth of the gospel we have proclaimed to you.***

He says,

"We entreat you; we are trying to persuade you to not turn your back on the grace of God. Do not receive the grace of God in vain."

In other words,

"We entreat you to so accept and embrace the truth of the gospel, to so follow that word that it will have its full affect upon your heart, and therefore within your life."

Paul says in 1 Thessalonians 2:13, he says of himself and of those who believed and embraced his message that, *"When we heard the Word of the gospel, we did not accept it, or receive and embrace it, as the word of man, but for what it really is: The Word of God, <u>which now mightily works within us who believe</u>!*

"So we entreat you," 2 Corinthians 6:1,

"…not to receive the grace of God in vain"

He says,

"Behold, now is the acceptable time, now is the day of salvation."

Verse 3 of Chapter Six says,

"We put no obstacle in anyone's way, so that no fault may be found with our ministry."

"We put no obstacle in anyone's way…"

Paul says in other words,

"We are committed to so promote the Word of truth, the truth of the gospel, the love of God, that there would be absolutely nothing

found in our ministry to cause you to stumble."

Let me tell you that your life is your ministry and your ministry is your life. There really is no way to separate ministry from real life. There really is no such thing as secular and sacred. Jesus didn't come and live a double life. He didn't live two lives: a Divine life - and a human life. No, He live one life, He lived His life as a human in union and fellowship with God.

Listen, your life and your ministry is so intertwined that there is no separation between the two. The day you stop separating the two you will realize that as you live your life in fellowship with God conscious of your absolute union with Him, ministry happens automatically, everywhere you go as you simply live your life

Listen again to what Paul said:

"We are committed to so promote the Word of truth, the truth of the gospel, the love of God, that there would be absolutely nothing found in our ministry to cause you to stumble."

If this is truly the way Paul and his team lived their lives in ministry, so that absolutely nothing could be found in their lives and ministry to cause these people to stumble, then *where do these obstacles and stumbling blocks in people's lives come from?*

Chapter 2

All Ministry Flows From the Love of God!

Let's turn to 2 Corinthians 4:1.

*"Therefore, having this ministry **as we have obtained the mercy of God**…"*

I want you to see that Paul's ministry, as well as our ministry, *if it is to be real ministry,* is the fruit of the impact of the truth of the gospel upon our hearts. It's the fruit of insight and understanding into the truth of the gospel, *into the love of God.* It is the fruit of God's grace in our lives.

Every single person's ministry, anyone who has a real ministry to people, is the result, the product, of the work of God in their hearts, in their inner man, through revelation knowledge into the truth of the gospel, into the love of God.

I say again: All real ministry is the result, is the product of the work of God in a person's heart and life.

Ministry is not something that you qualify for, because you've completed a certain course of study and received a special kind of certificate for it.

Ministry is the fruit of what God has accomplished **in your heart** through the gospel, through the love of God. It's the fruit of what God has accomplished in your life through revelation into the work of redemption through the influence of His grace.

Now Paul says,

"As we have this ministry, by the mercy of God, (by the working of God's grace) *...**we do not lose heart**..."*

You see, all these things that have come to Paul's ears could cause him to feel disheartened and discouraged, *but he was trusting in the grace of God. He was trusting in God Himself.* And so now he is speaking to the church, and he is saying, *"...**we do not lose heart!**"*

"We do not lose heart, for we have received a ministry by the mercy of God (We have been placed into the ministry, into God's own ministry, by the grace of God, by the influence of His love, by the influence of the revelation, by insight and understanding into the work of redemption, by His influence through that grace upon our hearts and within our lives)."

I know I am going a little back and forth between chapters here and what Paul had to say in various places, but I hope you can follow me.

If we go back there to 2 Corinthians 3:4, Paul says,

"Such is the confidence that we have through Christ!"

He says,

"Such is the confidence that we have through Christ towards God, not that we are competent of ourselves to claim anything as coming from ourselves, but our competence is from God!"

"...our competence is from God, who has made us competent to be ministers of a new covenant."

"...a new covenant, not in a written code, but in the spirit, for the written code kills, but the Spirit gives life!"

I want you to clearly see in this book *the integrity of the ministry God has called us into.* I want you to see *the integrity of that ministry, the integrity of your ministry!*

You see, your experience in Christ Jesus, your experience of the love of God, *because of your embrace of the truth of the gospel,* **is a ministry!** Not even one believer is called to just have a little private encounter with God. We are all called to be fountains of living water. *Every one of us is called to be a fountain of living water!*

The enemy would seek to close the faucet of your fountain. He would seek to so contradict the integrity of the gospel, the integrity of God's love, and the integrity of your ministry, so as to discourage you and make you feel that you're a failure. He wants to convince you that *you cannot possibly effectively communicate Christ.*

But the Scripture says, Paul says, the Spirit of God, the Spirit of Jesus Himself says,

*"**When that veil is removed,** (**when that deception, that hindrance is removed,**) **we all, with unveiled faces, behold as within a mirror, through the liberty of the Spirit, the glory of the Lord within us!**"*

And that glory, the love of the Lord, the joy of the Lord, the liberty of the Lord, the glory of the Lord, cannot be hidden. IT CANNOT BE HIDDEN! It begins to show forth, *and it has an impact!* But the enemy seeks to cancel the impact of that ministry that the Lord has given you, *that ministry of love and joy and liberty and life and glory coming forth from within you.*

Paul says in 2 Corinthians 4:2,

*"But we have renounced disgraceful, underhanded ways. **We refuse to practice***

cunning, and we refuse to tamper with God's Word..."

Do you see that?

"...We refuse to tamper with God's Word..."

In other words,

"We refuse to receive any other opinion about ourselves, any lie, any deception, any false identity, any lesser identity!"

"We refuse to accept any other message."

"We refuse to accept any method in ministry, whatsoever, that would seek to contradict the integrity of the Word."

"We refuse to practice cunning..."

We don't need to do that!

The message we both live in front of people and proclaim is powerful enough to change people's minds about God, to impact them and to totally change their hearts and minds and transform their whole being, their whole lives, amen.

Listen, God's truth, the truth of the gospel, the love and truth of God revealed in the gospel, is powerful! That truth is like a lion! All we need to do is open the cage, open the gate, and let it out. *It can take care of itself!* It doesn't need any defending; it can

43

stand on its own. Therefore we never need to get into fights or arguments. The Gospel is all about a quality, abundant life to be enjoyed and lived; it is not some intellectual thing, some religious doctrine that needs to be defended. *We simply need to proclaim the truth clearly; the truth of God's love and His work of redemption accomplished in Christ Jesus, so there can be no misunderstanding.* We can proclaim it with conviction and with accuracy and clarity, and it will take care of itself and do its own liberating work in people's lives!

"We can do nothing against the truth, only for the truth!" – 2 Corinthians 13:8

And so Paul says here, in 2 Corinthians 4:2,

"We refuse to practice cunning, and we refuse to tamper with God's Word…"

"But by the open statement of the truth, we commend ourselves to every person's conscience in the sight of God."

That means we will not allow any stumbling block or any obstacle to the integrity of the gospel to be placed in anyone's way *in the way we represent the gospel in our lives; through the way we live.*

Chapter 3

Life More Abundantly!

"And even if our gospel is veiled…"

Now Paul says here, in 2 Corinthians 4:3,

"…even if our gospel is veiled; even if some people just don't see it,"

"…it is veiled only to those who are perishing..."

Why are they perishing?

He says,

"In their case, the god of this world (this natural world, this natural dimension we live in) *has blinded the minds of the unbelievers…"*

Do you see that **it is only unbelief that causes that veil to remain?**

"Unbelief has blinded their minds, to keep them from seeing the light of the gospel, of the glory of Christ…"

The gospel is **all about the glory of Christ!**

The gospel is **the glory of God on display in Christ!**

Listen, the gospel is not four steps you have to take. The gospel isn't even some kind of definition of redemption. No listen, the gospel is **a revelation of the glory of God.**

What is the glory of God?

It's grasping the nature of God, it's grasping the truth that **God is love** *and that **God is your Daddy.***

That's what the gospel is all about; that's what *the glory of God* is all about! **It's being reconciled with God.** It's coming into abundant joy and abundant love and abundant living!

*"The thief comes to steal, and to destroy, and to kill, **BUT I HAVE COME** (says Jesus) that you might have LIFE MORE ABUNDANTLY!"*
— John 10:10

In other words, **so that your life might become the reflection of the life of God, of God's life, of abundant life, of the abundance of life, of what life is all about! That's God's promotion of His life! That's the reality of His glory!** *His abundant life, displayed in your life!*

Yes, all have sinned and fallen short of the glory of God. ***BUT we have all been justified.***

We have been brought back into that glory, into the glory we fell from, into His glory, by Jesus Christ, *as we embrace the gospel.*

2 Corinthians 4:4,

"Unbelief has blinded the minds of people; it is keeping them from seeing the light of the gospel, which is: the glory of Christ."

"The glory of Christ is: **the likeness of God.***"*

Christ is the likeness of God.

Mankind is hungry for God, *for the real God.* Not the religious, fabricated god, no: *the real God,* **the God who is love.**

And the gospel tells us that that God **who is love** wants to demonstrate to Mankind the reality of His image, the reality of His love, and the reality of His very person, *in a redeemed people.*

Listen, God wants your life to promote the gospel of His Son because of your encounter of His love in you; *that life more abundantly.*

2 Corinthians 4:5,

*"****For what we preach is not ourselves, but Jesus Christ as Lord.****"*

We preach His love! His life in us! The Christ-life! We preach Christ in us! His love in us! Him we preach!

"Christ in us, the hope of glory!"

"Him we preach!"

Paul says, *"We do not preach ourselves.* ***We preach Him as Lord.****"*

"Where He is Lord, there is real freedom!"

While I live my life under the dominion of His lordship, *I know the liberty of and the freedom of the gospel.* And so, there, in me, *you will be able to behold His glory.*

*"...****with ourselves as your servants for Christ Jesus.****"*

Verse 6,

"For it is the God who said, 'Let light shine out of darkness!' who Himself has shone in our hearts, to give the light of the knowledge, of the glory of God (in the face of a man) *in the face of Jesus Christ..."*

That same authority which created this world re-created the well-being of my spirit-being. Resurrection life entered my spirit-being and brought *'zoë'* - **life**, *where there once was death.* He re-created, re-generated, re-energized, and re-animated my inner-man, the well-being of my inner-man, by awakening faith in me, awakening His LIFE, His *'zoë'* in me, *awakening my spirit to His existence and to His love and to His life and to His reality.*

It is that same God, amen!

That same God that gave birth to the universe, that same God that gave birth to His glory in the face of a man, that same God that gave birth to His LIFE, to His image and likeness and to His glory in Jesus Christ, **that same God gave birth to His life and love and glory, in me.**

I share the same origin. I come from the same heart. It is that same God, amen. That God who is my origin, who is the source of my life, who brought me into existence, amen, that same God brought me out of death, out of darkness, out of that useless existence, into life, into His love and into His life again, in Christ Jesus!

Chapter 4

Treasure In
the Face of Christ

Paul says in 2 Corinthians 4:6,

"That same God, has shone into our hearts, to give the light of the knowledge…"

You see, my experience with God now has substance, *it has content and substance.*

It's not just some airy-fairy thing. It's not just some fairytale I swallowed, some cleverly devised little myth or fable I follow.

Listen, no, the substance of our glory that we share in Jesus is discovered in revelation knowledge. We have *this* knowledge of the glory of God **in the face of Christ**. *It's our treasure.*

Beholding Him *is our treasure, amen.*

That's where we get our substance from, *that's what fuels our experience and our encounter of God.* Our focus in these things now fuels our fellowship with God, amen. **It's the truth of the gospel. That revelation knowledge, the very knowledge of God revealed to us of who He is and who we are,** *is the*

substance of our fellowship with God. **It is the very fuel of our experience and encounter of God.**

What is the face of Christ?

The face of Christ is His Word revealed to your Spirit, ***the truth of the gospel revealed to your spirit…*** <u>***that Word***</u> **contained in the Scriptures** ***is the face of Christ.***

So when you hear the Scriptures being preached or when you read your Bible *and true revelation comes to you,* **you are looking into the face of Christ!**

When the Spirit of God gives you revelation into the truth of the gospel, **you are looking into the face of Christ!**

Sometimes, you know, we are trying to picture a Jew; we are trying to picture a man with long hair like we have seen Him in the children's Bibles. And we try to picture what He looks like and what He is like, **but God wants to break open the Scriptures for us and show us the face of His Son in there,** *so He can show us who* <u>*He*</u> *really is,* <u>*His*</u> *very heart, in the face of His Son.*

Paul says in 2 Corinthians 5:16,

"We at one time have known Jesus after the flesh, ***but we know Him thus no longer****,"*

Listen, God is not interested in giving us the exact features of how tall Jesus was, how handsome He was, what His body looked like and what His facial features were and all that. *Else, He would have made sure for it to be recorded in Scripture.*

But no, **God wants to show us the features of His spirit, of His heart, reflected in His face, reflected in His Word.**

And so, as we behold His Word in the Scriptures, as we behold His Word, as we behold this Word, as we behold this gospel, *as we behold this mirror,* a miracle happens in our spirit. A miracle happens to us. Transformation takes place; *we are changed into the same image,* and we can no longer live a lie. **The lie is undone, deception is dealt with.** We are conformed to the truth we behold in that mirror. That truth we behold in the gospel becomes a reflection in our heart, which shines forth in our being, *in our very lives.*

2 Corinthians 4:6,

"For it is the God who said, 'Let light shine out of darkness!' who Himself has shone in our hearts;"

"…to give the light of the knowledge, of the glory of God, in the face of Christ Jesus."

Hallelujah!

*"...**the knowledge of the glory of God, in the face of Christ Jesus.**"*

Let me tell you, people are not interested in theology, **but they can relate to the knowledge of the glory of God** *in the face of a man, in the features of a real person, in the features of a person not that dissimilar to them, not that far removed from their humanity*...**a person just like you and me!**

Quite often we have visitors from other countries that come through our place and sometimes they are not even that fluent in English. *But their spirit immediately relates to that glory of God they encounter in our meetings* **and see in us.**

I mean, from time to time we even get complete atheists or agnostics, or people from various other religious backgrounds coming through. Even the occasional Satan worshiper, or someone who is into witchcraft or something like that, and they can sit in on our meetings and think, *'Well, I've never been to any religious service or a meeting like this.'* **But something in their spirit** *bears strong witness* **to the integrity of God's love for them!**

God knows how to bear witness of Himself, how to speak for Himself, amen! God knows how to speak their language, *the language of the heart.* He knows how to speak to their hearts and say, *"You're in the right place!"* He knows how to gently minister to them by His Spirit, *how to impart and permeate their being with His love,* amen. Because He is not far from any one of us, amen. In Him we all live and move and have our being, amen, and He gives to all men life, breath, and all other things.

Is it really such a stretch for us to believe that God can communicate with someone's spirit, *even if they have not embraced His love and embraced His being and welcomed the reality of His person yet?*

God is fully capable of that and He does it all the time, amen. **He has been wooing them and drawing them with cords of love from day one of their existence.** How can any one of us respond to God and come to God *unless we are first drawn to Him by His Spirit, amen?!*

The term *"light"* is just a little parable to show us what that knowledge of God *does for us, what it means to us.* It's like light that is shot up into the night sky by the military or some other person, *to illuminate the darkness.* It's like the light that comes up on the horizon in the morning sky and it transforms the darkness into light, *it turns the night into day.* It's like I have been stumbling around in the darkness and tripping over stuff *and suddenly the light is turned on for me and I can see clearly now.*

That light of God, that knowledge of God, says Paul, *deposited a treasure within us.*

2 Corinthians 4:7,

"We have this treasure (this light, ***"the knowledge of the glory of God"****) …**we have this treasure in earthen vessels"***

Paul says, *'Now listen man, don't get distracted by the color, or the shape, or the history of this earthen vessel, or even the shape it is in, amen.* **Because the attraction of your life is not in your good looks, amen. The attraction of your life is in the substance of the knowledge of the glory of God!***'*

In other words, **what makes your life attractive is not your past performance or how clever you are, what a big shot you are, how handsome you are, how ugly you are, or whatever.**

No listen, the attraction of your life *is the Spirit of Jesus,* the glory of Jesus, residing and abiding in your spirit, and reflected throughout your whole being, in your very life!

This is the treasure we have in these earthen vessels, amen.

Now notice what Paul says here in Verses 7 & 8,

"We have this treasure in earthen vessels, ***to show that the excellence of the power belongs to God and not to us****."*

In other words, **it is not the achievement of the flesh, amen. It is not the achievement of the flesh,** *but the achievement of God in us!*

God wants to *'achieve'* something in you! And He wants that *achievement'* to be reflected in your life.

And hallelujah, if God could create out of a miserable mess, this beautiful planet we live on (the Bible says, *"The earth was void, it was without form,"* and yet out of it God created the beauty of nature.), **just imagine what beauty God can create in a person's spirit even though it, too, has been void at one time; filled with darkness, in a confused and miserable state.**

Chapter 5

Applying The Treasure!

Paul says here now in 2 Corinthians 4:8,

"We are afflicted in every way..."

Now that almost seems out of context, and one almost want to stop the chapter there at Verse Seven and say, 'Well, that was a very nice chapter, let's just underline and emphasize only up to there.'

"We have this treasure in earthen vessels,"

…**wonderful treasure that we are, and that we have!**

And now let's just walk with this treasure through life and hold it close to our chest and make sure we don't get any dents or scratches on it. And let's just try and preserve this treasure so we can make it to heaven unscathed. And then, one day, in the sweet by and by, we will finally be able to enjoy this treasure in heaven.

No man, listen, what is the purpose of this treasure that we are and that we have?

You see, this gospel we preach, this gospel, *this knowledge of the glory of God in the face of Jesus Christ,* is not a fairytale. It is not an airy-fairy teaching, it's not a teaching that you can only apply one day when you get to heaven. **No, it is the Word of God, the will of God, *revealed* for you, for today, for NOW!**

God wants us to see that this treasure has purpose and meaning *for your life and my life, here on planet earth!*

How do I apply this treasure, practically, in my life?

"We are afflicted in every way..."

Why would you be afflicted? Why would anyone face affliction?

Because someone, the evil one, the enemy of our faith, is after that treasure.

Jesus Himself said in the Scriptures, in Matthew, in His parable of the sower, that *persecution arises on account of the Word.* **It breaks out against you and *comes against the Word.***

So, here I am, I've heard the Word, I've heard the truth of the gospel, and the conviction of that truth came into my spirit. And I rejoice before Jesus that I was made a new creature in Him, in His death, burial and resurrection, and that I am now seated with Him in heavenly places, fully accepted and embraced in the bosom of our Father. I rejoice in the fact that I have been fully restored in Him to my original design, to the image and likeness of God, to that divine nature which is within me, within my spirit. And I praise God for my new future in Him here on planet earth, and that I am going to heaven one day.

But here I am going around the next bend in the road, around the next corner on life's journey, *and suddenly everything just seems to collapse around me.*

You see, affliction comes to us all. We have this treasure, *but affliction comes,* and Paul says, *"…**in every way**."*

I mean, it seems to just come from every direction sometimes, and everywhere I turn, there it pursues me and finds me again.

But now Paul says in 2 Corinthians 4:8,

"We are afflicted in every way, **BUT we are not crushed**"

This has everything to do with our fellowship and interaction with that treasure. It has everything to do with the integrity of that treasure we are, and carry, and treasure here in our inner-man.

That word *"**crushed**"* in the original Greek is a very interesting word. The one translation of that verse says,

*"We are afflicted in every way, **BUT we are not restrained.**"*

That word *"**crushed**"* means **to be crowded together into a narrow space, a restricted space; to be cramped into a little place.**

So that means that **the enemy wants to reduce your sphere of influence, he wants to reduce the potency and the potential of your ministry.** So the enemy comes to restrict the impact of your ministry, of your life. Your life is your ministry, amen. *You* have received a ministry. God gave you a ministry.

In 2 Corinthians 5:17 & 18 Paul says,

"Therefore, if anyone is in Christ, the new creation has come, (it's a reality)*: the old has gone, the new is here! All this is from God, who has reconciled us to Himself through Christ **and gave us the ministry of reconciliation.**"*

So, I have this ministry, I have this treasure, and you have this ministry, you have this treasure.

But now we're afflicted.

Paul says,

*"We are afflicted **in every way, BUT we are not crushed!**"*

He says,

*"We are perplexed also, **BUT not driven to despair!**"*

You see, the enemy comes against you because of that treasure, because of the potential of that treasure, or because you fully understand the significance and the value of the treasure you have; you truly grasp the knowledge of the glory of God and what it means, not only for you, but for your neighbor, *and you become compelled by the love of Jesus in you to share it with them*.

So because of these things, when the enemy comes against you, *he wants to drive you into a narrow environment where it **feels** to you that there is no more room to be free, to just live, and move and have your being ...and I feel so restricted, because now suddenly everything has collapsed around me.*

But there is encouragement for us right here in Paul's words. The Spirit of God says through Paul.

'**Hey listen, take courage!**'

'**With this treasure as your focus, as your treasure, fully embraced within your bosom, you will not be crushed!**'

'**In fact, beholding this treasure and holding on to this treasure in your heart, you will come into a new broad place, an unrestricted space!**'

He says,

*"…perplexed, **BUT NOT DRIVEN TO DISPAIR!**"*

The phrase *"**driven to despair**"* is made up of two little words in the original Greek, and it literally comes from the word *'**poros**'* which means **away**. The word that is used is actually the word *'**aporos**'* meaning **no way**. It means I come to a place and there is just no way left to go. I cannot go any further. Every way I try to go, everywhere I turn, there are major obstacles. It's like this big wall that totally blocks my way, or this big black cloud round about me, and I cannot see my way through.

Paul says, in other words, that we come into difficult situations like that. Even though I have this treasure, I come into a difficult situation *where everything seems dark around me.*

But now the Spirit of God says through Paul,

*"…we are not '**exaporao**'…"*

That means **we will never come to the place where we are stuck. We will never come to a place where there is just no way.**

It might seem for a moment that there is no way out. But God says, *'I WILL MAKE ANOTHER WAY!'*

"With my God, I'll leap over a wall, and I'll break through a troop!"

Psalm 18:19 says,

"He brought me forth into a broad place! He delivers me because He delights in me."

Listen, God delivers you because He delights in you!

He wants you to live in a broad place, in an unrestricted place!

"He brought me forth out of this narrow place, into a broad place!"

So I throw myself on Him, on His love for me, and I trust Him! I trust Him to bring me out and to deliver me!

In spite of all that is coming against me, I trust Him to keep working through me and to keep speaking and witnessing for Himself! To keep working with me in my ministry to others, confirming His own Word, confirming His own message through me, His own glory, exhibited in me, through my life, *with signs, wonders, and miracles!*

You should read my books: *"Jesus said: 'I will build My Church!'"* and *"Zoë"* to understand these things more fully.

Chapter 6

Hinds' Feet on High Places

What is that narrowness He is talking about? I mean, what brings about that narrowness, that restrictive place, *restrictive living?*

In 2 Corinthians 6:12 Paul says,

"You are not restricted by us, but you are restricted in your own affections."

Obviously these people said to Paul,

'No, Paul, we simply can't receive your ministry anymore because of this and because of that and because we can't fully embrace what you are saying anymore.'

They were held back and restricted by something. They felt they couldn't receive Paul's ministry and so they in their minds had come up with millions of reasons why they couldn't embrace His gospel anymore.

But Paul said to them, *'No,* **the gospel we preach is not from us,** *this is not about us, our ministry to you.* **The Word we preach has been commended by God.***'*

He says, *'our gospel has integrity, it is not sometimes yes and sometimes no. **It is yes and amen in Christ Jesus!**'*

Paul says,

'There is no way you are restricted by us. You are restricted only by your own affections!'

You see, those affections of the flesh, we sometimes want to cuddle up to and cling to as idles, is a lie.

They're a lie!

Because they promise us a tremendous experience and then suddenly, when it's all said and done, and we buy into it, *we find ourselves locked up in a situation.*

We are restricted by our own desires!

And we have all known that way of living, the narrowness of that way, living within the confines and restricted limits of the flesh. But listen, *God wants to bring us into the limitless environment of the spirit.*

Psalm 18:19 says,

"He brought me forth into a broad place! He delivers me, because He delights in me."

Notice what He says in Verses 33 and 36,

"You make my feet like hinds' feet and set me secure upon the heights."

"You gave a wide place for my step under me, and my feet did not slip."

Listen, that mountain deer has an ability that a giraffe does not possess… ha… ha… ha… It has a specific adaptation to its environment. It can climb the highest, steepest, mountains, *but its feet don't slip.*

"You make my feet like hinds' feet, and set me secure upon the heights."

"You gave a wide place for my step under me, and my feet did not slip."

God, through His Word, through the truth of the gospel, through the truth of His love, through the faith that comes from Him, gives you an ability to tread upon the high places, the treacherous place, when suddenly you find a mountain in front of you, and you wonder, *'How am I ever going to be able to overcome this? How am I ever going to be able to pass through this treacherous valley, this restrictive place, or over this thing, this unsurmountable mountain in front of me?'*

But it is then in that situation that God begins to speak to you. The abiding Word within you begins to speak to you, and Christ begins to dwell afresh and anew in your heart through faith, and you become strengthened with might by His Spirit in

your inner-man, and God imparts to you a new ability within you to stand secure in Him, in the middle of that situation.

Look at the next verse there, in Second Corinthians,

2 Corinthians 4:9,

*"We are persecuted, **BUT not forsaken!**"*

*"We are stuck down, **BUT not destroyed!**"*

God wants us to learn how to keep our emphasis and our focus *on the treasure.*

He wants us to grasp the ability of the full measure of that treasure.

Through fellowship with Him, by His Spirit, in the truth of redemption, God wants to enlarge our hearts to appropriate, to grasp fully, to thoroughly understand and comprehend and embrace every dimension of that treasure we have and hold in our hearts.

Chapter 7

The Glorious Liberty of the Children of God

Let's go to Romans Chapter Eight quickly. In Verse Twenty-One it speaks of *the glorious liberty of the children of God.* Where the Spirit of the Lord is, *wherever that Spirit is Lord,* there is liberty, there is freedom, amen. Now I've come to know Jesus, and I think,

'Wonderful liberty!'

But then, suddenly I find myself afflicted, I find myself perplexed, and things come against me, and I wonder,

'What in the world is this liberty all about? I thought that when I become a Christian everything is just going to be a bed of roses. I mean, I was told everything is just going to be abundant living, abundant life!'

Hey listen, it is abundant life, it is abundant living! But that abundant living, that abundant life is in the treasure.

Romans 8:21,

*"…the **glorious liberty** of the sons of God."*

What is the *"**glorious liberty**"* of the children of God?

Romans 8:29 says,

"Those He foreknew, He also predestined (or pre-designed, or pre-planned for them) *to be conformed to* (or to be jointly-formed in) *the image of His Son."*

That is God's pre-designed plan, both God's design of your life, and destiny for your life. It is God's destination that He had already set for you from before time even began.

God's pre-destined plan is to conform Man to the image of His Son, simply because it was His pre-destined plan to jointly form Mankind, every individual, in the image of His Son at the beginning of everything.

That is why it has been pre-determined; God pre-planned for Man, He pre-planned for you, from the beginning, He planned for you to be restored back to His image.

He did this in Jesus.

He first jointly-formed you in the image of His Son before time began. And then after the fall, in time, in Jesus, He came and rescued you and restored you back to what you fell from.

In that marvelous work of redemption He restored you, He jointly-formed you again in the image of His Son.

Ephesians 2:10 clearly says that,

"We are His workmanship, created in Christ Jesus, for love, and the good works that flow from that, which He prepared beforehand (which He pre-designed, and pre-planned and pre-destined) *for us to walk in..."*

He pre-destined and pre-designed us for His love!

He pre-planned for us to know and to walk in that love!

To know and to walk in sonship!

To <u>be</u> in the image of His Son.

He wants us to be conformed to the image of Jesus, *that image of sonship revealed in Jesus, in the face of Christ Jesus,* **so that we may know and walk** *in that same love, the love of the Father Himself,* **which Jesus knows and enjoys and walks in in His sonship.**

Verse 30 of Romans 8 says,

"In order that He might be the first-born among many brethren."

Hebrews 2:11 says,

"He is not ashamed to call us brethren!"

Go ponder on that one until it explodes in your spirit! I guarantee that once you grasp it, it will blow your mind, *and your walk with God will never be the same again!*

Romans 8:30,

"...For those whom He pre-destined, He also called, and those whom He called, He also justified, and those whom He justified, **He also glorified!***"*

Can you see with me that the revelation of righteousness, the revelation of being made the righteousness of God in Christ, there in that work of redemption, *is to bring you into the glory of God?!*

God restores us in Jesus and to Jesus, because He wants to bring us to the glory of life more abundantly in Him.

So what is that life all about?

Even though I live in the midst of a crooked and perverse generation, where there is conflict, and affliction, and contradiction, *and people are trying to persuade me contrary to the faith of God,* **I have this treasure within me, in my heart, seated and lodged deep within my spirit, within my consciousness.** *And it springs forth, it bears its fruit of life more abundantly, and I overcome everything that comes against me.*

I am more than a conqueror, through Him who loves me, and gave Himself for me, and to me!

That's why Romans 8:31 now says,

"What then shall we say of all of these things that come against us?"

*"**If God is for us, who can be against us!**"*

*"**He who did not spare His own life, but gave Himself up for us all, will He not also, with Christ Jesus, give us all things?**"*

Chapter 8

God Is For Us! Not Against Us!

In Romans 8:33 Paul continues to say,

*"Who then shall bring any charge against God's elect? **It is God Himself who justifies them!**"*

"Who is there left to condemn?"

*"**Is it Christ Jesus** who died; The One who was raised form the dead and is at the right hand of God, and indeed is our intercessor, by His very person?"*

In other words, *"**Do you think Jesus, or the Father, will condemn you?**"*

He begins in the very beginning of this chapter; Romans 8:1, *with the final conclusion to his argument in all the previous chapters of His letter to the Romans,* with the final, **NO** to this question.

He says in Romans 8:1,

*"There is **therefore now no condemnation** to those who are in Christ Jesus!"*

Because we have already been justified in Him, in that successful work of redemption, amen!

So next time, when affliction comes, or when spiritual persecution comes, don't think, *'Oh, here we go, God is acting up and He is judging me again, and condemning me.'* **No man, listen, He took the judgment upon Himself. He did it in your place!**

"If God is for us…"

"Who can be against us?"

The biggest problem Mankind could ever face would be *to have God as our enemy!* **But I have good news for you,** *God is not our enemy!* **He has never been, nor will He ever be our enemy, amen!**

Just imagine for a second God actually turning against you. How preposterous, how absurd. There would be absolutely nothing and no one left on this planet if God was to ever turn against us!

But you see, that is exactly what the enemy wants you to think. That's exactly what the devil wants to persuade you of. **He wants to lie to you and tell you that you are ugly, and that God doesn't like you anymore, and that God wants nothing to do with you,** *that you have failed Him.* But Satan is nothing but a liar from the beginning; he is the father of lies, *of deception!*

Listen, Paul says here …God Himself says here, in Romans 8:31,

"**<u>SINCE</u> God is for us, who can be against us?**"

And when did God decide to be for us?

From the beginning, amen! When He pre-designed us and pre-destined us, amen!

When did He decide to demonstrate that love that is ever towards us? **When did He decide to demonstrate His immense love for us?** I mean, when did Jesus die for us?

When we were yet sinners, amen! While we were still sinners He died for us!

He didn't wait for us to become nice people before deciding to die for us and demonstrate His love for us!

No, He made us nice people, amen. He didn't wait for us to choose Him, He chose us, amen.

He took the initiative while we were lost, while we were hostile towards Him, while we wanted nothing to do with Him.

That's exactly when He took the initiative.

You see, He had already chosen us and loved us and decided to die for us and give His life up, just to be with us, and to reconcile us to Himself!

He made His mind up about these things before time even began.

Ephesians 1:4 says that *"He chose us in Christ before time began, before the foundations of the earth were laid, before the fall of the world even."*

He had already made His mind up, and He had already chosen us in love, before the fall, therefore not even the fall was going to get Him to change His mind, *because His decision was from the heart!*

He chose us in love!

Now in the light of that,

"Who shall bring any charge against God's elect!"

I want you to see that we are called *to persuade people of this!*

But the truth is, you cannot persuade anybody else *if you are not first persuaded yourself!*

I tell you, the enemy knows that and He wants to stop your ministry *by bringing things against you.* And he brings things against you *to bring you to a place where you doubt and you hesitate and you are not quite so sure of the love of God and what He has done for you anymore.*

But when I walk in the persuasion of the integrity of my salvation and I know that I know that I know *God is not condemning me.* When I am sure, I mean, I remain convinced that *God is for me, He is not against me, He is for me, that He is on my side;* then and then only am I in a position *to persuade others also* of the same thing.

You see, when I become that persuaded in the depth of God's love for me, in the enormous love of my Daddy God for me, then I can begin to allow my life to so reflect the beauty and the love of Jesus.

And then also, I can effectively, and in my very person, in my conversation and in my conduct, *contradict every lie that the devil uses to hold people in bondage.*

"It is God Himself who justifies me and glorifies me!"

Hallelujah!

Romans 8:34,

"Who is there left then to condemn me?"

*"**Is it Christ Jesus** who died; The One who was raised form the dead and is at the right hand of God, and indeed is our intercessor, **by His very person?**"*

By no means, amen!

The Father doesn't condemn us and neither does Jesus! There is no one left to condemn us, amen!

Hallelujah!

Verse 35 says,

"Who can possibly separate us from the love of Christ?"

It is possible to be separated from the love of Christ, amen. But who can separate me from that love? Only me, amen!

I alone can separate myself from the love of Christ and reject it and refuse to have anything to do with it; to have anything to do with Him, amen. It's called **choice**, amen.

"What can separate me from the love of Christ?"

"Shall tribulation, or distress…"

This word *"distress"* is the same one we have looked at before in 2 Corinthians 4:8 where it speaks about **coming to a narrow place.**

"What can separate me from the love of Christ?"

"Shall tribulation, or distress, or persecution, or famine, or nakedness, or peril, or sword?"

You see, all these things come to contradict the Word of God, to contradict the gospel, *to contradict the love of God.*

Listen, these things are things we all experience or can experience from time to time in a very practical way in this world. While we live on this planet, any one of these things can befall us, especially when we allow ourselves to be inspired and motivated and controlled by the love of Christ and we give ourselves over to His influence and go around proclaiming and sharing and making known the truth of the gospel.

Paul says these things are there, they are a reality, and they come against us, sometimes very practically in our own lives. In our own experience of life they come against us *and they come to contradict and to try and cancel that Word, to cancel the gospel in my heart and life. They come against me to try and cancel and stop my ministry!*

Paul says, *"We experience these things just as it was written that we would."*

He says, in Verse 35,

"It is just as it is written, 'We are being persecuted for Your name's sake; we are being killed all the day long. We are regarded as sheep to be slaughtered.'"

Who regard us as sheep to be slaughtered?

Our enemy, the enemy of our faith does, amen. Satan does!

Who else regard us as sheep to be slaughtered?

Those who misunderstand our message, those who reject our message and come against us and persecute us, amen.

They quite often don't even realize that they are being used to do the devil's bidding, amen.

But here in Verse 37 Paul says,

"NO!"

I want every one of you reading this book to look your circumstances in the face, to look the devil in the face, to look that persecution you are going through in the face, and to say, ***"NO!"***

Say it out loud!

NO!

And why do I want you to say it out loud?

Because you see, the devil wants to tell you that, *"YES,"* you are going to be cut off from God, and God doesn't like you anymore; *you have failed God.* And, *"YES,"* you stand condemned, and you are no good, and *you are not going to make it!*

But Paul says ...God says,

Verse 37,

"NO! In all these things you are more than conquerors through Him who loves you!"

So the next time the devil tries to put you in a situation financially where it seems there is no way out and you feel, *'I am so distressed!'*, set your mind on this scripture here, bring it to your remembrance. Bring to your remembrance where Paul says,

*"What shall separate us from the love of Christ? Shall tribulation or distress or whatever else ...***shall it separate me from the love of God? NO!***

God says, **NO! IT SHALL NOT!**

Listen, NOTHING shall separate you from the love of God! NOTHING can separate me from the love of God! So, here you are and your marriage is threatened. Or here you are and you find yourself with a situation in your body, and suddenly your health and sometimes your very life is threatened, and the devil is trying to speak to you, and your mind is screaming at you,

'Oh my goodness, I am about to die! I am going to die of this thing, I am going to die young, and gosh, I still wanted to do so many things, but I am about to die of this thing!'

Listen, the Bible says, *"NO!"*

The Scriptures say, *"NO!"*

The devil says, *'YES, you are going to die young. You are going to die, I've been trying to tell you, but you aren't listening.'*

He is trying to persuade you. You see, it's a battle of persuasion. But you need to answer back,

'Yes, devil, you are right, **I am not listening to you!** *And no, you are wrong, it's a lie, I am not about to die. I am not going to die of this thing. I will not die. I refuse to die'*

Paul says, *"NO!"*

God says, *"NO!"*

He says I don't have to die! He gave Himself for me and to me so I don't have to die. The same Spirit that raised Christ from the dead now dwells in me. I abide in Him and Him in me, *and He sustains my life, amen!*

He says, *"No! In all these things I am more than a conqueror, through His love, through Him who loves me!"*

The devil is the father of lies and he is trying to persuade you *contrary to these things all the time.* The devil says, *'You are not going to make it,'* **but God says, *"NO!"***

Now, you can agree with either one, it's your choice! **BUT AS FOR ME, I am going to agree with the truth of the Gospel, I am going to agree with the Word of God, I am going to agree with God, I am going to come into agreement with the One who loves me, and is for me, not against me!**

Romans 8:37,

*"No! **In all these things** we are more than conquerors!"*

Through the shed blood of Jesus Christ, amen, *we are more than conquerors!*

Chapter 9

Hold Fast The Confession Of Your Faith!

What makes the knowledge of Jesus a treasure? What makes this knowledge of redemption a treasure?

It's value, amen!

How is value measured?

By its usefulness, amen!

You see, the value of gold is not just in the beauty of the substance. Gold's value is not just in its shine, amen.

The real value of gold is in **what it can purchase!**

The value to God of you being a regenerated person *is not just so you can enjoy the nice vibes of the presence of God.*

No matter how wonderful that is, God wants to use that reflection of that reality of His life, of His indwelling in you, *to keep you free and to liberate other people at the same time!*

When depression and melancholy comes against you and tries to persuade you contrary to the fruit of the spirit, contrary to the liberty and the joy of the spirit-life, when it comes and tries to persuade you that you don't have any peace or any reason for joy, that you are just a looser and a miserable old failure of a person, *you better take authority over that thing and tell your mind to shut up.*

You better say to it,

'No listen, I will not be separated from the love of Christ! I will not allow this contradiction to the knowledge of the love of Christ to continue within my thinking!'

*"No, in all these things **I am** more than a conqueror, **through Him who loves me!**"*

I am more than a conqueror, **through the knowledge of His steadfast love!** Through the knowledge of my worth and my value to Him! He loves me, amen! HE LOVES ME! PERIOD!

HE LOVES ME!

We, therefore, have more than enough energy deposited within us *to overcome in any situation!*

*"...**through Him who loves us!**"*

The secret to 2 Corinthians 4:8 & 9, the secret of, *"...being afflicted in every way, BUT not crushed, being perplexed, BUT not driven to despair, persecuted, BUT not abandoned and forsaken, struck down, BUT not destroyed..."*

The secret of that is discovered ***in your personal measure of that treasure, your personal measure of the love of God that has impacted your heart, and abides there.***

Our treasure truly is our persuasion in the love of God *which nothing can separate us from.*

Listen, God is as committed as can be to your life through His love for you!

God has given us His love, imparted and awakened in our hearts as the guarantee of His Word for your life, as a sure warranty of the truth of His gospel, which directly applies to you, to your life!

Romans 8:35 & 37,

"Who shall separate us from the love of Christ?"

"NO! In all these things we are more than conquerors through Him who loves us!"

In Romans 8:38 Paul says,

"Now I am sure..."

That word *"**sure**"* can also be translated as **fully persuaded.**

Paul says,

"Now I am persuaded!"

"I am convinced!"

*"**I am fully persuaded** that neither death, nor life ...nor angels, nor principalities ...nor things present, nor things to come ...nor powers of any kind ...nor height, nor depth ...nor anything else in all of creation, will ever be able to separate us, from the love God, in Christ Jesus our Lord!"*

Ha... ha... ha... Hallelujah! Isn't that good!?

The enemy comes and he tries to create an environment of dust around you, just a dust cloud, nothing more, just a smoke-screen and mirrors, nothing more, just mist and fog, nothing more, amen, *just a bunch of lies and deception, amen.*

Oh, don't get me wrong, it may appear so real, and **feel** so real. And it may threaten your very life, but he is no match for God!

Ha... ha... ha... Hallelujah!

And guess what? The enemy is no match for those whose faith is active and alive either. **The devil is no match *for the believer*, amen.** Those circumstances are no match for those who trust in the Almighty God, the God who specializes in accomplishing the impossible, amen!

The enemy is always at work **to try and get you persuaded, contrary to the love of God, contrary to redemption truths, contrary to those things, contrary to those realities,** *contrary to that scripture we just read.* But when I am persuaded, when I am convinced, when I am fully persuaded, that faith of God comes alive within me, *it creates a shield around me.* It creates an environment around me that makes it impossible for the devil to break through. His lies and deception simply will not work on me. His efforts are neutralized, amen.

I love the way Paul thinks and writes.

Ha… ha… ha… Hallelujah!

I love the way He begins his closing statement. He begins with the worst possible thing that can happen to you, and he says,

"For now I am convinced that neither death…"

I just love that! The very worst thing, the number one thing the enemy has held as his number one weapon against all of mankind, against every single individual: DEATH.

Paul says,

"Now I am convinced …I am persuaded…"

Now remember that Paul speaks from experience of such things, he speaks from

93

revelation. He is not busy with wishful thinking here, some kind of mystical, unattainable concept. Paul has not only a revelation of the resurrection of Jesus Christ, but he has a personal revelation of the power of the resurrection of Jesus Christ. He reminds us in several places in the New Testament Scriptures in his writings to the saints that *the sting of death is destroyed in the cross, in the death of Jesus Christ, and that death no longer has any virtue. It no longer has any power over the saints.*

*"…neither death, **nor life**…"*

Some people are even more scared to live than they are to die, amen.

Romans 8:38,

*"**For I am convinced that neither** death, nor life, nor angels, nor principalities* (whether they are human governments or demonic forces)*, nor things present, nor things to come…"*

You might be, right now, in a present situation that is quite bad. It is quite narrow and restrictive and threatening. And you might be experiencing a lot a fear right now. That fear in your mind is, *'If it is this bad now, I wonder how bad it is still going to get?'*

No! Hey listen, *"…nothing in the present, nothing to come, **no power, no principality, no height, no depth, no length, no extent to which things can sometimes go to, nor*** *anything else in all of creation is able to separate you from the love of God!"*

Paul says,

"I am convinced …I am persuaded …fully persuaded …neither death, nor life, nor angels, nor principalities, nor things present, nor things to come, nor powers of any kind, nor height, nor depth, nor anything else in all of creation, will ever be able to separate us from the love God in Christ Jesus our Lord!"

Hey listen; this is the largest guarantee of all guarantees!

"…no height, no length …no measure of any circumstance, no matter how big it is…"

Paul is saying,

"Come on, how big is your problem? Measure the height of it, measure the size of it, measure the extent of it, measure the length of it, measure the durability of it, measure the depth of it, measure the severity of it, **go ahead and measure it all you like.**

BUT I AM HERE TO TELL YOU: IT CANNOT OUT-MEASURE GOD'S LOVE! **IT CANNOT OUT-MESURE GOD'S ABILITY TO KEEP YOU!"**

That understanding, that revelation, that knowledge, *that is what our joy is in!* Jesus says, *"***You CAN rejoice, FOR I <u>HAVE</u>**

OVERCOME THE WORLD! *Even though you have persecutions and the like in this world."*

Listen, resurrection life out-measures death every time!

This resurrection life that we have received in Him out-measures every single thing that the devil can possibly bring against us and throw at us.

That's why Isaiah, prophetically seeing our day says this in Isaiah 54:17,

"No weapon formed against you shall prosper."

He says, Isaiah 40:2,

"Comfort, yes, comfort My people, say unto them that their warfare has ended!"

He says, *"No weapon formed against you…"*

He doesn't say, *"The enemy will never form any weapons against you…"*

No, he says, *"No weapon formed against you shall prosper!"*

The enemy is constantly at work trying to frustrate your life. But the Lord says to those who trust in Him and rely on His love and on His grace that, *"No weapon formed against you shall prosper!"* **God takes all things that come against you and He turns it around and *He makes things work out in your***

favor. He turns it around and *makes it work for your good.*

Listen what gives God the freedom, the confidence to declare and prophesy these things? I mean, He knows we are frail human beings in the flesh. He knows this crooked and perverse generation will try and walk all over us and undermine us and work against us and persecute us. He knows we are dealing with real devils and demons in this world that want to steal from us and destroy us and kill us.

Sometimes we think Jesus should have prayed,

"Father, I pray that you do not keep them in this world, but that you would take them out of this world..."

"...as quickly as possible, Father, before they are totally overcome by the devil and by the world, and lose the struggle and backslide, and end up even worse than ever before!"

No. Jesus prayed,

"Father, I do not pray that You would take them out of this world, but that You keep them from the evil one, **that You keep them through your truth. Your Word is truth!**"

Can you see Jesus' confidence in the ability of His Word, in the ability of His truth within us, the truth of His love, to keep us?!

Can you see with me that His Word, the truth of the gospel, the truth of His love for me, produces within me an ability to stand against all the wiles of the evil one?

And not just to stand, but to shine as lights in the midst of that crooked and perverse generation!

The Word, the truth within us, the love of God that has taken up residence within our hearts, the Spirit of Christ that now permeates our being is at work within me, both to will and to do of His good pleasure.

This whole thing works just like a tick collar that you place on a dog. That chemical, that white powder, the influence that comes from that collar which rubs off on that dog becomes a shield; an invisible barrier, a saturating influence within every cell of that dog's skin, so that that dog can now go and run around outside in that same tick-infested field and be just fine! The ticks may bite, but they fall off and they die; they don't stay on that dog long!

Ha... ha... ha...

One of my favorite songs lately is one that is used in a dog commercial: *There may be bugs on some of you mugs, but there ain't no bugs on me!*

Hallelujah!

The Word of Christ, the truth of the gospel, produces an ability within me to preserve me, it comes to me and brings that ability into my spirit, amen, it empowers me; it is my weapon, amen.

It equips me and empowers me against every weapon the enemy forms against me.

My spirit is weaponized… ha… ha… ha… ready to take on and defeat anything that comes against me, anything the enemy may throw against me, any weapon he may form against me and launch at me, amen!

*"This is the victory that overcomes the world, **even our faith!**"*

This is exactly how we are able to stand in the midst of any affliction, any contradiction, every affliction possible, amen, ***because I am persuaded!* I am convinced of the love of God for me.** I am convinced that God is love! I am persuaded that God is for me, not against me! I am convinced that He is on my side! **I am fully persuaded!**

"I am convinced that neither death, nor life, nor anything else..." And here I go, I am listing every possible weapon that the enemy can form against me, ***and I come to the conclusion, to the conviction, that they won't prosper.*** They simply won't be able to prosper against me, they won't prosper, *and I am convinced, I am persuaded,* **I am fully persuaded!**

If it cannot separate me from the love of God, then it cannot separate me from the power of God in operation in my life, and that means that *my deliverance is close at hand! I am fully persuaded of this!*

Chapter 10

Give the Devil No Place!

I am fully persuaded. And by that persuasion I overcome the evil one!

But listen, I am telling you now, and I am warning you that *if you are not persuaded, if you are not fully persuaded, they will prosper.* The devil will have your lunch and eat it too, and pop the bag right in front of you, and you will just have to stand there and watch and take it all in, and there will be nothing you can do about it!

You see, the devil knows that principle too. The enemy knows that if he can manage to succeed, *if he can manage to persuade you contrary to the love of God, contrary to the truth of the gospel...*

Because you see, he is also trying to persuade you. He is constantly trying to persuade you contrary to these things. He is constantly trying to sow his seeds of doubt and fear, and of unbelief into you. And he knows that if he can manage to sow these things into you *and succeed in persuading you contrary to the truth of the gospel,* then he has you.

Then you can become his prey; then he can have his way with you and do whatever he wants to with you.

He is trying to persuade you contrary, and he will use anything and everything. This is exactly what was happening there in Paul's letter to the Corinthians. The devil used all kinds of ideas and opinions contrary to the truth that these people had already embraced, and he began to use it to criticize Paul's ministry in their minds, and the truth of the gospel he was preaching.

And as those people began to adopt those contrary thoughts and ideas, those opinions began to be a negative influence upon their hearts and it began to threaten the integrity of Paul's ministry, the integrity of Paul's work among them, the very integrity of the work God had already done in their spirits when they first heard the Word of truth, the gospel of their salvation. It began to threaten the work of the ministry, it began to threaten Paul's ministry among them and in that whole region.

Can you see that, can you see the enemy's strategy; can you see how the enemy works?

And listen, I am not saying all this so that you can start focusing on the devil now, and make a big deal of him, and see a devil behind every bush, and blame the devil for every circumstance and situation you encounter in your life.

If you feel like you have to now try and deal with the devil and constantly fight with him, *then I can already tell you that you are in error and you are trying to put a defeated foe back into business!*

The devil has already been dealt with. He has already been defeated and disarmed at the cross in the work of redemption. He has been stripped of his power in the work of redemption. He is simply no match for God or for you, amen.

'Then how do I deal effectively with the devil when he does show up in my life and come against me, brother Rudi?'

Sometimes you have to address the enemy, just like Jesus had to, and bind a devil when it manifests, and put an immediate stop to its activity. *But that happens very seldom.* **So stop fearing the devil and making so much of him!** We share in Christ's executive authority. We have been seated together with Christ in the heavenly places, in a place of authority. Far above, not just above, but far above, out of the reach of, every principality and power and might and dominion, amen.

And so, now the best way to deal with the enemy, *the best way to resist his influence,* **is to ignore him.**

The fight is real simple; ***it's a fight of faith, it's a wrestling match of persuasion.***

The enemy is trying to get you riled up, he is trying to get your attention, he is trying to get you to focus upon him and to wrestle with him and to fight with him, *to give him all your attention,* so that you **focus** upon him, and he appears bigger and stronger and unbeatable, and in that way he can **move you away from your conviction, from your strong stand, from your full persuasion in the truth and in the love of God,** and he can get you *discouraged* and he can *succeed in persuading you contrary to the truth* **and get your eyes completely off of Jesus** and on to him and on to yourself and on to your circumstances.

No, the best way to deal with him effectively is to look away from what the devil is doing ...to look away from your circumstances, to take your attention and focus off of yourself and your struggles **and to focus instead upon Jesus and upon His love for you!**

Look away unto Jesus, the author and finisher of our faith, and let the battle be the Lord's.

Quit struggling with your struggling and get caught up in the abundance of His love, in the abundance of the provision God has made for you in Christ!

It is real simple. You just simply continue to remain persuaded about the truth of the gospel, about the love of God <u>and focus all</u>

*your attention on these things ...Focus all your attention on your Daddy's love for you, on the fact that He is for you, not against you, and that He is on your side ...*Simply hold on to your persuasion about these things. Simply remain *fully persuaded!*

That is the best way to resist the devil and to have him flee from you! **Simply remain steadfast in the faith!**

And the God of peace will soon crush Satan underneath your feet.

If you stand steadfast and immovable in these things, and you remain fully persuaded in your faith, in the faith of God, in His Word of truth that abides in your heart, in your spirit, God Himself will confirm His Word. He will confirm the gospel, the truth of the gospel, *the truth of His love for you,* with signs, wonders, and miracles!

Living in constant victory is as simple as that!

God wants us to learn how to maintain our focus in the truth of the gospel, how to remain fully persuaded in His love *and then how to stir one another up.*

Remember Cain, when God came and confronted him about what happened to Abel? Do you remember Cain's response? Cain asked, *"Am I my brother's keeper now?"*

I want us to realize that **we are indeed one another's keepers.**

In the unity of the Spirit and in the bond of peace we need to maintain the environment of the immeasurable love of Jesus.

Chapter 11

The Immeasurable Love of Jesus!

Let quickly also go to Ephesians 3:17. Paul prays for the believers and this is his prayer,

*"I pray that Christ may dwell in your hearts through faith; that you **being rooted and grounded in** love…"*

Being rooted and grounded in love **means to be fully persuaded!** It means that no wind that comes against me, no contradiction to my person will uproot me and pull me out of the love of God.

Paul continues, he says,

"I pray that Christ may dwell in your hearts through faith; that you being rooted and grounded in love **may be empowered to comprehend fully**…"

That word *"**comprehend**"* means **to fully possess, to fully appropriate.**

What's the use of knowing a lot of scriptures that you can quote off by memory or knowing a lot of spiritual religious principles *that you cannot even appropriate in your day to day life?*

"I pray that Christ may dwell in your hearts through faith; that you being rooted and grounded in that <u>love</u>, **may be empowered to fully comprehend (to fully possess, to fully appropriate)** *with all the saints, the breadth and the length and the height and the depth; to intimately and fully know the love of Christ which surpasses knowledge."*

Listen, that's our treasure: *full possession, fully, intimately knowing the love of Christ.*

We are talking about heart knowledge here, *full persuasion; full possession!*

We are talking about a knowledge that *way surpasses understanding.*

It's of another dimension, it's of a spirit dimension, it's of a faith dimension; *it's of a heart dimension, amen.*

Listen, your mind can get tired of 1+1=2. You can so easily get bored with that knowledge. There is a vast difference between knowing about love, and being fully in love with someone! You can get bored with knowledge, but love, the language of the heart, *that conviction and persuasion of the heart,* is another matter altogether. *It surpasses knowledge.* Your heart speaks the language of love, an intimate language that the mind sometimes cannot even comprehend.

You see, your spirit, your heart, cannot get enough of, *'I love you'*. Your spirit, your heart, understands that language perhaps more than any other language! **The love of Christ which surpasses knowledge is what our spirits feasts off of. It's the bread of life, and the living water;** *it's what your inner-man of the heart lives off of.*

Ephesians 3:17,

"I pray that Christ may dwell in your hearts through faith; that you being rooted and grounded in <u>*love*</u>*, may be empowered to fully comprehend with all the saints what are the breadth and the length and the height and the depth;* <u>*to intimately and fully know the love of Christ*</u>*, which surpasses knowledge'*

Listen, that's our treasure. **That treasure of the love of Christ** which surpasses knowledge. Just like a diamond has facets, it **has depth to it, it has dimensions to it. And those dimensions out-shine and out-measure every persuasion which seeks to contradict God's Word, which seeks to contradict and undermine the truth of the gospel.**

But you see it comes by revelation, the impartation, the depth of it comes through revelation knowledge. And that revelation, the dimensions of it, the depth of it, the largeness of it, the full measure of it, is maintained within the environment of, the fellowship of, the saints.

Quite often the depth of love, the largeness of it, cannot be explained; *it can only be experienced!*

Chapter 12

Maintaining a True Heart

I want us to finish in the book of Hebrews, so let's take a look at it over the next couple of chapters. This whole book of Hebrews has but one theme: **God wanting to persuade Man of His love!**

Hebrews 6:17 says that God desires for the heirs of the promise **to be more fully persuaded; more fully convinced!**

What is it that He wants us to be persuaded in?

He wants to fully persuade us in *the reality of our redemption*. He wants to persuade us in the reality of it, *the significance of our salvation*.

Why?

So that we won't neglect such a great salvation.

So he says there in Hebrews 4:16 that we may now draw near **with a confident heart, with a new confidence, because we are reconciled to God.**

Listen; there is no more condemnation, amen. God does not hold our trespasses against us. God doesn't have any ill will, or any negative vibes in His heart towards us.

Instead He has a joy in His heart when He looks at us, when He looks at humanity. He has joy because He knows He paid the highest price to buy us back, to redeem our minds out of darkness, to win our hearts back to Him through the extravagant display of His love.

And now the Scriptures say to us; I mean, just look with me quickly at what we are to do now, how we are to respond to that.

First of all, Hebrews 10:22 says,

*"Let us draw near now with a **true** heart; **in full assurance of faith**..."*

That means **being fully persuaded.** *To draw near with a **true** heart means* **to be fully persuaded.** *Full assurance of faith means* **to be fully persuaded.** Our hearts must be fully persuaded in this new and living way. That means: we must not allow the enemy of our faith, the accuser of the brethren, to condemn us and keep us outside of the presence of God.

We cannot afford to live this life outside of a genuine love relationship with God, outside of an intimate friendship and fellowship with God.

*"Let us draw near now with a true heart; in full assurance of faith, **with our hearts sprinkled clean from an evil conscience**…"*

Don't let a sin-consciousness rob you of the love and the life and the joy and the liberty you enjoy in Jesus!

A sin-consciousness will immediately bring you into a narrow place again and you'll feel restricted and you'll feel condemned and all bound up and you can no longer enjoy liberty in your relationship with God. Listen; the blood of Jesus perpetually cleanses us from all sin!

Hebrews 10:23 goes on to say,

"Let us hold fast the confession of our hope, (of our faith) ***without wavering**…"*

In other words, **being fully persuaded.** He is showing us how to maintain our confidence, how to maintain our persuasion, how to maintain our intimate love-affair with Him.

He says, *"…holding fast **the confession of** our faith..."* That word ***"confession"*** is the word *'**homologao**'* in the original Greek and it means **to speak and to say the same thing as God says; to come into absolute harmony with the thoughts and the words of God.** That means **my confession continues to be what God says in the truth of the gospel.**

The accuser of the brethren, the enemy of our faith, the devil himself comes and he says, *'Yes, yes, yes, you are going to be separated.'*

But then you answer back and you say, *'No! The Scriptures say I won't. God says, 'No! I won't!' God says that nothing can separate me from the love of God!'*

So, I am maintaining that persuasion, I am maintaining that confession.

Even when sickness or symptoms, or whatever thing, comes against my body or against my finances or against my marriage or against my mind, or whatever, then God says, *"NO!"* The Scriptures say, *"NO!"*

And the devil is still trying to say, *'Yes, yes, yes, you are not going to make it,'* **BUT God says, *"NO!"*** The Bible says, *"NO!"*

So, because God says, *"NO,"* when the Bible says, *"NO,"* then I say, *"**NO!**"*

When the Bible says, *"Yes,"* then I say *"**Yes!**"* **because God says, *"Yes!"***

That's what maintaining is all about: **holding fast to the confession of my faith *without wavering!*** You see, I'm just agreeing with God! My mind and my emotions might get all confused and begin to amplify those symptoms or those circumstances and begin to think along with those things. ***BUT I'm allowing the truth of the Gospel, I'm allowing the Spirit*** *of truth, I'm allowing the Spirit of God within me, I'm allowing God Himself, I'm allowing His love to rule over my mind and over my emotions from out of my heart, to renew my mind to think in line with God's thoughts.*

So that when God says, *"Yes!"* **I also say,** *"Yes!"*

When God says, *"Yes!"* **then I say,** *"Amen!"*

"Let us draw near now with a true heart; in full assurance of faith, **with our hearts sprinkled clean from an evil conscience***…"*

"Let us hold fast our confession of faith **without wavering, knowing that He who promised is faithful***…"*

Why can we be so bold as to hold fast to our confession? Why can we be so bold in maintaining full persuasion?

Because God is directly, intimately involved! God is involved in His promise! His faithfulness is linked to His promise!

*"**He who promised is faithful***…"*

God is watching over His Word to perform it, to make it good!

Listen; God is not a man that He should lie! God doesn't change His mind, amen! He doesn't ever need to repent! He has made

His mind up! God's heart has made up His mind concerning you!

His Word is not sometimes yes and sometimes no! His Word, the truth of the gospel, is yes and amen in Christ Jesus!

The intensity of His love with which He loves us is not going to diminish. Ever! There is no dark side to God! There is no *'other side'* to the love of God! No! God is love. He loves me and you!

In the gospel, in the truth of the gospel, in the truth of the love of God, God is not holding out a carrot in front of us to try and draw us into deception! No! God is faithful to His promise! God is committed to the integrity of His eternal purpose concerning you, and concerning your life! He has called us into the fellowship of the Son!

God wants you to keep enjoying the maximum life you can ever live, a life in union with Him, the maximum life you can possibly enjoy, a life in fellowship with Him ...regardless of circumstances, even in the midst of affliction, even in the face of persecution!

Listen; God wants your life to be beautiful in spite of all these things! God thinks you're beautiful! God wants you to explode with His joy ever abounding in your spirit! God wants you to live the life of a conqueror! He wants you to live a life of being more than a conqueror! He wants you to live an abundant, victorious life, a life of being more than a conqueror over every affliction, over every persecution, over every circumstance, over everything that comes against you!

Imagine yourself that way!

Just imagine living that kind of a life!

Just imagine the kind of life Jesus lived!

And you can do it, amen, because He has deposited His own nature within you! He has deposited Himself within You! He abides in you and you in Him!

Your life is hidden with Christ in God! Safe and secure in the bosom of your Father! Wrapped up and embraced in the arms of your Daddy! In the arms of your Lover! In the arms of Him who loves you with an eternal, unending, immense, and intense, passionate love!

God knows He can count on the influence of His truth, and on the influence of his love, and on the influence of His nature, and on the influence of His Spirit in you!

That is why He doesn't want us caught up in religion, in stale old religious principles, but in the encounter of His love and of His life in us, in the interaction with that life in us. His incorruptible seed has given birth to His life in me, and therefore His enablement, His very own ability to overcome is awakened within my heart.

His ability is my ability, amen! His power is mine to draw from, amen!

God wants us to live in the reality of an intimate love relationship with the living God, amen!

I have said all these things simply to help you maintain the victory that Jesus has already given you!

I am saying all these things to help you *to be continually persuaded of His love, and of His nearness, and of His faithfulness, and of your victory in Him, and of the devil's defeat!*

So, let us draw near to God, let us draw away from an evil-conscience, a sin-consciousness, and let us hold fast to our confession of His love and of the truth of the gospel, *for God is faithful!*

Chapter 13

The Fellowship of the Saints

And now Hebrews 10:24 & 25 says,

*"…and **let us consider how to stir up one another to love and good works;**"*

*"…**not neglecting to connect with one another, to meet together, to enjoy genuine friendship and fellowship with one another**…"*

He says,

*"…**let us encourage one another all the more!**"*

He says,

*"…**in so doing we see the day approaching**,"*

*"…**we see the influence of darkness being undone and the influence of the kingdom go forth!**"*

Amen!

Hallelujah!

*"**The true light is already shining and darkness is passing away!**"* (1John 2:8)

The writer of Hebrews says we are responsible for one another's faith. Our calling is not just to reach the lost with the love of God, with the truth of the gospel, but it is also *to preserve* **the fellowship of the saints.** *To preserve* **the unity of the Spirit.** *To preserve* **the bond of peace.**

These things are all talking about the same reality, amen. The reality of family. God is building a family, amen. He is not building a *"church"* or anything else. No! He is building a family; His family, the household of Faith, the children of God. *And we are responsible for one another's faith!* We must learn how to help preserve one another's faith, amen!

*"...**let us consider how to stir up one another to love and good works**,"*

*"...**not neglecting to connect with one another, to meet together, to enjoy genuine friendship and fellowship with one another**..."*

*"...**let us encourage one another all the more! We see the day approaching, we see the influence of the kingdom growing and gaining momentum!**"*

Hebrews 10:35 & 36 continues,

*"**Therefore do not throw away your confidence**..."*

The enemy is constantly trying to steal your confidence, *to take your confidence away.* And when you've lost your confidence, *you are no longer fully persuaded.* **And when you are no longer fully persuaded *you are being separated from God, not in reality from God's perspective, but in your heart.***

Listen; you can never be separated from God amen. Separation is a lie. There is no such thing as being separated from the presence of God. God is in you, amen. He has come to make His abode with you, amen. So, you can never get separated in reality, but you can be separated from God in your heart. You can lose track of the truth and lose track of His love, and lose track of His nearness and His indwelling, amen.

And the devil is trying to bring that sense of separation into your heart to where you feel separated, to where you no longer feel fully accepted and connected, to where you no longer feel confident, to where you are no longer fully persuaded of His love and of these eternal, redemption realities. And when you are no longer fully persuaded *you are being separated by the enemy.*

That is why Hebrews 10:35 & 36 says here,

"Therefore do not throw away your confidence, which has a great recompense of reward."

"You have need of endurance, so that after having done the will of God you may receive what is promised."

He says, ***"You have need of endurance!"***

That sounds to me like **maintaining full persuasion!**

What does it mean when it talks about, *"after having done the will of God?"*

It is talking about ***maintaining full persuasion!***

You see, when you are maintaining full persuasion, you are doing the will of God! When you maintain full persuasion, *you enter into what is promised; you enter into the experience of it. You enter into what it means to intimately know the love of Christ which surpasses understanding.* And that my friend is entering into the will of God for your life! *You enter into what the truth of the gospel affords us, you fully enter into what Jesus made available for us to enjoy in the work of redemption!* That is what the will of God for you is all about!

That's what living in the will of God gets you! That's what full persuasion gets you! Being more than a conqueror, living in constant victory, living in constant, intimate, sweet fellowship with God, *no matter what!*

You see, that is why it is so important **to maintain a positive environment.** That is why it is so important **not to neglect the fellowship of the saints.**

Paul says that some have gotten into the habit of doing this, of neglecting the fellowship of the saints, and it is dangerous. That is why I want to encourage you even now, in this book, to look around you. In the town you live in, in your region even, where you live, connect with other believers, especially other believers who understand these things we are talking about, and get to know them, so that you can learn what family is all about; so that you may together encourage one another.

If there is a group like that in your area that meets together as a church (I am not talking about religious organizations now and boring dead religious churches ...ha ...ha ...ha ...go to them too, amen, and share the love of God and the truth of the gospel with them, amen. And God may grant them eyes to see too, if they want it, if they embrace the truth of the gospel, amen.) But look around in your area and find believers that fully embrace the truth of the gospel and live in the freedom of the Spirit. And if they meet as a group, make friends with them and go to their meetings, show up at their prayer meetings, and show up at their Word schools, and schools of ministry, so that there can be a mutual encouragement of one another, **so that there can be a conversation and a genuine fellowship that is building,** *so* *that your hearts can be knitted together in love and genuine friendship.*

Because you know, we can sometimes so easily be influenced by the devil, and then we get robbed. I mean, it is sometimes so easy to come up with even a stupid little excuse to neglect these things. Like, for instance, waking up on a day when we know our friends are meeting, the believers are gathering together and meeting this morning, the family is gathering, *but I don't **feel** like going. So I think to myself that that is reason enough not to go, and so I don't go. And I end up going less and less,* and the enemy uses stupid little reasoning like that **to rob people** all the time and to mess with people and *to get them to do what he wants them to do,* **so he can keep them weak and out of fellowship and isolated enough to mess with them some more.**

But now you see, when you've got a real friend, a genuine brother or sister who bothers to call you and say, *'Hey, are you going to be at the meeting today? You know, I would love to see you. And just let me know if you don't have a ride, I am more than happy to come and pick you up. But let's go for it; let's go to that meeting together.'*

You see, they may annoy me, but I am being encouraged. I am being stirred, *contrary to what my body and my mind and my emotions are trying to dictate to me.*

My mind and my emotions may say, *'I am tired,'* and my body may want to be lazy and enjoy some more sleep. **So it is trying to persuade me contrary to what God, through the Scriptures, is encouraging me to do.**

And now I have a brother or a sister who is working with God helping Him uphold His Word in my life, and speaking the truth of the gospel to me. They might be a little bit of a nuisance to me, but in a little while I'll stop being perturbed at them and I might even want to bless them back and be a genuine blessing to them also, **for because of them I yielded and was brought into the blessing of the environment of fellowship.**

You see, God truly wants to bless you but you need to maintain a positive environment and you need to be there for others and help them do the same.

The enemy is working all the time. He is working over me; he is working constantly to try and neutralize that environment, trying to contradict the truth, the encouragement of the Scriptures, trying to contradict the love of God and the blessing that comes from standing firm and maintaining a constant environment of being fully persuaded.

But as we resist him, he must flee from us. As we understand that we stand responsible for one another to help maintain that strong environment of

fellowship, that strong environment of encouragement, that strong environment of full persuasion in the love of God and in the truth of the gospel, we give the enemy no place and he finds no more room to maneuver, no platform to operate from in our hearts and lives.

I say again: **We are responsible for one another.** You are just as capable of being responsible and you are just as responsible for your brother or your sister as any pastor is or anyone else.

And listen I am not talking condemnation and obligation here now; *I am talking genuine love, amen.* We get to do these things, there is no *'have to'*s here, only *'get to'*s ...ha ...ha ...ha ... it is a huge privilege and an honor. We get to serve one another in love, amen. It's because of love; *it's the fruit of genuine love, amen!*

As we maintain these things, as we maintain the unity of the Spirit, as we maintain the bond of peace, as we maintain our fellowship with one another, as we maintain full persuasion together, *we will together develop an enthusiasm in our spirits and we will begin to see ourselves as ministers of the New Covenant, as ministers of reconciliation, reconciling people to God, embracing them ourselves as family, embracing them in love!*

And in our hearts, in the inner imagination of the heart, we will begin to see ourselves ministering, we will see ourselves ministering to others, because of that strong impartation of love and faith, because of that strength that is imparted, we will begin to see ourselves ministering to others, and ministering to the world, and then we'll begin to do it. We will live to persuade people, to impact them with love, and to impart the truth of the gospel and the love and the life of God to them and we'll become skilled at it, effective at it, amen!

And we won't have to become religious and dogmatic, and use clever arguments and human wisdom and man-made little myths and fables to try and argue with them and persuade them.

Because we are not trying to argue with them as if we have dominion over their faith, *but we will present ourselves merely as helpers* **of their joy. And our joy and our love for Jesus, and that abundance of life and liberty we enjoy in Him will bear such strong witness with them, with their hearts. And their own hearts will speak to them and let them know that they need what we have.**

We don't walk as mere men, with the strength of the persuasion of our arguments, we don't walk as dogmatic religious people, **but we walk in love, we walk in the demonstration of love, in the demonstration of the power of love, and in the demonstration of the power of the Spirit, in the demonstration of the truth of the gospel.**

God bears witness of Himself and of His love in us, and of His life in us, and He bears witness to the truth of the gospel, and of His love for people, for them as individuals, with signs and wonders, and miracles following.

So, we want to live lives that persuade people in the integrity of the gospel, and we want to keep everything away from us that would cause a stumbling block; that would cause people to trip and stumble over the simplicity and the profound truth of the gospel.

God wants us to be committed to that, as believers God wants us to be committed to that, and in our fellowship and as a church, or as a group that meets together also.

God wants us to have a strong commitment in these things, because of love. He wants us to commit to so live that we promote, not undermine, but promote the gospel of Jesus Christ.

In closing, I want to urge you to get yourself a copy of *The Mirror Bible.* It is the best translation of the Scriptures from the original Greek that I have ever read, because it rveals the heart of God and Paul's gospel the clearest. It's available on-line at: www.Amazon.com and several other book sellers.

If you want me or someone from our team to come to where you are, *anywhere in the world,* and give a talk or teach you and some of your friends *about the gospel message and these redemption realities,* simply contact us at www.LivingWordIntl.com Or you can always find me on Facebook.

If your life has changed as a result of reading this book, *please write to me and let me know.*

I would love to share in your joy *so that my joy in writing this book may be full!*

"That which was from the beginning,

which we have heard **(with our spiritual ears)**,
which we have seen **(with our spiritual eyes)**,
which we have looked upon **(beheld, focused our attention upon)**,
and which our hands have also handled **(which we have also experienced)**,

concerning the Word of life,

we declare to you,

that <u>you also</u> may have this fellowship <u>with us;</u>

and <u>truly our fellowship is with the Father</u> <u>and with His Son Jesus Christ.</u>

And these things we write to you that your joy may be full."

- 1 John 1:1-4

About the Author

Rudi & Carmen Louw together oversee: Living Word International.

They also travel and minister both locally and internationally.

Rudi was born and raised in the country of South Africa, while Carmen grew up in Cortland, New York.

They function in the ministry of reconciliation (2 Corinthians 5:18-21) and flow strongly with the Holy Spirit and His anointing to teach, preach, prophesy, heal, and whatever is needed to touch people's lives with the reality of God's love and power.

God has given them keen insight into what He has to say to mankind in the work of redemption concerning the revelation and restoration of humanity's true identity.

Therefore they emphasize THE GOSPEL: IN CHRIST REALITIES, the GRACE of God, the WORD OF RIGHTEOUSNESS, *and all such eternal truths essential to salvation and living the CHRIST-LIFE.*

They have been granted this wisdom and revelation into the knowledge of God by the resurrected Spirit of Jesus Christ, *to establish and strengthen believers in the faith of God, and to activate them in ministering to others.*

Not only are people set free from the poison and bondage of sin, condemnation and all kinds of intimidation, (upheld, strengthened and reinforced by age old religious ideas born out of ignorance) **but many are brought into a closer more intimate relationship with Father God, as Daddy**, through accurate teaching and unveiling of the gospel message, prophetic words, healings and miracles.

Rudi & Carmen are closely knitted together with many other effective Christians, church fellowships, and groups of believers who share the same revelation and passion **to impart the truth of the gospel to others,** *and so to impact and transform the world we live in with the LOVE and POWER of God.*

www.ingramcontent.com/pod-product-compliance
Lightning Source LLC
Chambersburg PA
CBHW071127090426
42736CB00012B/2033